Google Chrome Made Easy

A Practical Guide for Everyday Users

Tech Trends

Google Chrome Made Easy

TABLE OF CONTENTS

Google Chrome Made Easy

Google Chrome Made Easy

Google Chrome Made Easy

The History of Google: From Search Engine to Tech Giant

Google, now a global technology powerhouse, started as a humble research project by two Stanford University students. Over the years, it has evolved into one of the most influential companies in the world, shaping the way people interact with information, technology, and each other.

---

1. The Early Days: From Stanford Project to Startup

Google's roots can be traced back to 1995, when **Larry Page** and **Sergey Brin**, two PhD students at Stanford University, met and began collaborating on a research project. At the time, web search engines like AltaVista and Yahoo! relied heavily on keywords to rank websites, but Page and Brin believed there was a better way to organize and present web search results.

1.1. The Creation of BackRub (1996)

In 1996, Larry Page and Sergey Brin began working on a project called **BackRub**, which aimed to develop a search engine that analyzed the relationships between websites rather than just keywords. BackRub was unique because it used a new algorithm called **PageRank**, which ranked web pages based on how many other pages linked to them. This concept was revolutionary at the time, as it treated a link as a "vote" for the page's importance.

BackRub operated on Stanford's servers for over a year, but its growing popularity began taking up too much bandwidth, prompting the need for a more scalable solution.

1.2. Google is Born (1997-1998)

In 1997, Page and Brin decided to rebrand their search engine from BackRub to **Google**, a play on the mathematical term "googol" (1 followed by 100 zeros), symbolizing their goal of organizing vast amounts of information on the web. The domain name **google.com** was registered on September 15, 1997, and the following year, the Google search engine officially launched.

On September 4, 1998, Google was incorporated as a private company, and its headquarters was established in a friend's garage in Menlo Park, California. At this time, Google was still a search engine, but its clean interface, accurate results, and innovative approach quickly gained popularity.

2. The Rise of Google: Search Engine Dominance (1999-2004)

2.1. Investment and Growth

In 1999, Google received its first major investment of $25 million from venture capital firms **Sequoia Capital** and **Kleiner Perkins Caufield & Byers**. With this influx of cash, Google was able to move its headquarters to Palo Alto, California, and hire more employees. By the end of 1999, Google was processing over 500,000 searches per day, a number that would quickly grow.

2.2. The Google Toolbar and Advertising Innovations

In 2000, Google introduced the **Google Toolbar**, a browser plugin that made it easier for users to search without navigating to the Google homepage. The same year, Google introduced **Google AdWords**, its online advertising platform. AdWords allowed businesses to advertise on Google's search results pages through a pay-per-click model, revolutionizing online advertising and creating a new revenue stream that would fuel Google's growth.

2.3. Becoming the Web's Go-To Search Engine

By the early 2000s, Google's PageRank algorithm and streamlined interface had made it the world's most popular search engine, surpassing competitors like Yahoo! and AltaVista. In 2004, Google was processing over 200 million searches a day. Its dominance in the search market was now firmly established.

---

3. Google Expands: Diversifying Beyond Search (2004-2010)

As Google solidified its dominance in the search engine market, the company began expanding its services and diversifying into other areas.

3.1. The Google IPO (2004)

In 2004, Google went public, offering its initial public offering (IPO) on August 19. The IPO raised $1.67 billion, giving Google a market valuation of $23 billion. The company's founders, Page and Brin, retained majority control through a unique stock structure. This financial success allowed Google to make significant investments in both innovation and acquisitions.

3.2. Gmail, Maps, and Other Key Products

2004 was also the year Google launched **Gmail**, a web-based email service that offered users 1 GB of storage, which was revolutionary at the time compared to competitors like Yahoo! Mail and Hotmail. Gmail's simple interface and ample storage capacity quickly made it a popular choice among users.

In 2005, Google introduced **Google Maps**, a web mapping service that provided driving directions, satellite imagery, and street maps. Google Maps was soon enhanced by the launch of **Google Earth**, which allowed users to explore virtual 3D representations of the planet. Both products further solidified Google's role as an information provider.

During this period, Google also introduced several other key products, including **Google News**, **Google Scholar**, and **Google Analytics**, extending its influence in web search, information gathering, and online marketing.

3.3. YouTube Acquisition (2006)

In 2006, Google made one of its most significant acquisitions by purchasing **YouTube** for $1.65 billion in stock. YouTube, a rapidly growing video-sharing platform, provided Google with a massive user base and positioned the company as a leader in online video content. Today, YouTube is one of the largest platforms on the internet, further enhancing Google's dominance in the digital space.

4. The Android Revolution and Mobile Expansion (2007-2014)

By the mid-2000s, the rise of mobile internet and smartphones was becoming evident, and Google recognized the need to diversify into mobile technologies.

4.1. Android Acquisition and Growth

In 2005, Google acquired **Android Inc.**, a small startup that was developing an operating system for mobile devices. Two years later, in 2007, Google officially launched the **Android** mobile operating system, an open-source platform that allowed device manufacturers to customize and innovate. Android quickly gained popularity, becoming the dominant mobile OS worldwide.

The launch of the **Google Play Store** (originally Android Market) further helped Android grow, as users could download apps and games from the platform. With the rise of Android, Google cemented its place in the mobile world and created a multi-billion-dollar ecosystem that would later integrate with its services like Gmail, Google Maps, and YouTube.

4.2. Chrome Browser and Chrome OS

In 2008, Google launched the **Google Chrome** web browser, which quickly gained popularity due to its speed, simplicity, and efficiency. By 2012, Chrome had overtaken Microsoft's Internet Explorer to become the world's most popular web browser. Chrome also served as the foundation for **Chrome OS**, a lightweight operating system for laptops and desktops known as **Chromebooks**.

---

5. Google's New Era: Alphabet Inc. and Beyond (2015-Present)

5.1. Alphabet Inc. (2015)

In 2015, Google restructured itself under a new parent company called **Alphabet Inc.**, a holding company that oversees Google and its other ventures, including its research divisions

(Google X), life sciences (Verily), and self-driving cars (Waymo). This move was intended to provide greater transparency to investors and give Google more flexibility to innovate outside its core search and advertising businesses.

5.2. Google Cloud and Artificial Intelligence

During this period, Google made significant investments in **cloud computing** through **Google Cloud** and developed artificial intelligence (AI) technologies. AI tools like **Google Assistant** and **Google Translate** began incorporating machine learning algorithms to improve performance and user experience.

5.3. The Expansion into Hardware

In recent years, Google has expanded into hardware with the launch of products like **Google Pixel** smartphones, **Google Home** smart speakers, and **Nest** smart home devices. These hardware offerings, combined with Google's software and AI capabilities, position the company at the forefront of the smart home and connected devices markets.

---

6. Google Today: A Global Force

Today, Google is synonymous with the internet. It processes over **3.5 billion searches** every day, and its services—ranging from Gmail to Google Drive to YouTube—are used by billions of people worldwide. Google's influence extends far beyond search, shaping industries such as advertising, mobile operating systems, cloud computing, artificial intelligence, and hardware.

Google's parent company, Alphabet Inc., has a market value of over $1 trillion, making it one of the largest companies in the world. Despite challenges related to privacy, data usage, and regulatory scrutiny, Google continues to lead innovation in the tech space, working on projects ranging from quantum computing to self-driving cars.

Introduction to Google Chrome

Google Chrome is one of the most popular web browsers in the world, known for its speed, simplicity, and versatility. Whether you're completely new to web browsing or transitioning from another browser, Chrome offers a seamless experience across devices.

What is Google Chrome?

Google Chrome is a free web browser developed by Google that allows users to access and interact with websites, online applications, and multimedia content. Released in 2008, Chrome quickly gained popularity for its clean user interface, fast performance, and focus on providing a secure and user-friendly web experience.

Unlike older browsers that prioritised a more cluttered layout, Chrome introduced a minimalist design that puts the web content front and centre. It is built on an open-source project called **Chromium**, which ensures continual innovation and improvement.

Key Characteristics of Google Chrome:

- **Speed**: Chrome is optimised to load websites and web applications quickly, making it a favourite for users who demand fast browsing.
- **Simplicity**: The interface is minimal, with an easy-to-navigate toolbar, address bar (Omnibox), and a few essential buttons for managing tabs and settings.
- **Security**: Google Chrome includes built-in features that protect users from phishing attacks, malware, and other security threats. Regular updates ensure

that users are always running the safest version.

- **Cross-Platform Functionality**: Chrome syncs seamlessly across all devices, meaning you can access your bookmarks, history, and saved passwords from any device with Chrome installed.

Key Features and Benefits

Google Chrome is packed with features designed to improve the browsing experience for users of all skill levels. Whether you're using Chrome for casual browsing or more advanced tasks, it offers powerful tools to make your experience smoother, safer, and more efficient.

1. Speed and Performance: Chrome is known for its impressive speed, from loading web pages to running complex web applications. Its **V8 JavaScript engine** ensures faster script processing, while **DNS pre-fetching** predicts and loads links before you even click on them.

Chrome's streamlined architecture also reduces the strain on system resources, making it faster than many other browsers.

2. Omnibox (Combined Search and Address Bar): One of Chrome's standout features is the **Omnibox**—a unified space where you can type both website URLs and search queries. Instead of switching between a search box and an address bar, Chrome's Omnibox automatically understands whether you're searching for a website or entering a URL. It also provides suggestions based on browsing history, bookmarks, and search predictions.

3. Tab Management: Chrome makes it easy to manage multiple tabs at once. You can open as many tabs as you need without slowing down the browser. Chrome also includes options for **pinning tabs, grouping tabs**, and **muting specific tabs** that are playing audio. These features help keep your browsing organised and less chaotic.

4. Syncing Across Devices: With a Google account, Chrome enables **syncing** across multiple devices—whether you're using a desktop computer, laptop, tablet, or smartphone. Once logged into your Google account, Chrome syncs your bookmarks, browsing history, saved passwords, extensions, and even open tabs across all devices.

5. Security and Privacy: Chrome is constantly updated to fix vulnerabilities and improve user protection. It features **Safe Browsing**, which warns users when they try to visit potentially dangerous sites. Chrome also has an **incognito mode** for private browsing sessions that don't save your browsing history, cookies, or site data.

6. Extensions and Customization: The Chrome Web Store offers thousands of extensions and themes that allow users to customise their browsing experience. Whether you need a productivity tool, an ad-blocker, or even a visual theme, Chrome lets you tailor the browser to your preferences.

7. Automatic Updates: Chrome automatically updates in the background, ensuring that you always have the latest features and security patches without needing manual intervention.

8. Developer Tools: For more advanced users, Chrome includes a suite of developer tools that allow website developers to inspect and debug websites, monitor performance, and experiment with code in real time.

Installing Chrome on Different Devices

Google Chrome is available for a variety of platforms, including Windows, macOS, Android, and iOS. Here's how you can install Chrome on these devices:

Installing Chrome on Windows

1. **Download Chrome**:
    - Open any web browser on your computer (such as Microsoft Edge).

- Visit the official Chrome download page at google.com/chrome.
- Click the "Download Chrome" button.

2. **Install Chrome**:
   - Once the ChromeSetup.exe file is downloaded, click on it to start the installation.
   - Follow the prompts to complete the installation process.
   - After installation, Chrome will automatically open, and you can start browsing.

3. **Optional: Set Chrome as Default Browser**:
   - After installation, Chrome may ask if you want to set it as your default browser. If you agree, Chrome will open all web links by default.

Installing Chrome on macOS

1. **Download Chrome**:

- Open Safari or another browser on your Mac and visit google.com/chrome.
- Click "Download Chrome," and the .dmg file will start downloading.

2. **Install Chrome**:
   - Open the downloaded file (googlechrome.dmg).
   - Drag the Chrome icon into your Applications folder.

3. **Open Chrome**:
   - After installing, open the Chrome browser from the Applications folder or the Launchpad.

4. **Set as Default Browser**:
   - Chrome will ask if you'd like to set it as the default browser for all web links. You can choose to set it or keep your current default browser.

Installing Chrome on Android

1. **Open the Google Play Store**:
   - On your Android device, open the Play Store app.

2. **Search for Google Chrome**:
   - ○ In the search bar, type "Google Chrome" and select it from the results.
3. **Install Chrome**:
   - ○ Tap the "Install" button to download and install Chrome on your device.
4. **Open Chrome**:
   - ○ Once installed, open the Chrome app from your home screen or app drawer.

Installing Chrome on iOS (iPhone/iPad)

1. **Open the App Store**:
   - ○ On your iPhone or iPad, open the App Store.
2. **Search for Google Chrome**:
   - ○ In the search bar, type "Google Chrome" and select it from the list.
3. **Install Chrome**:
   - ○ Tap "Get" to download and install Chrome.
4. **Open Chrome**:

- ○ Once installed, open Chrome from your home screen.
5. **Optional: Set Chrome as Default Browser (iOS 14 and above)**:
   - ○ Go to **Settings** > **Chrome** > **Default Browser App**, and select **Chrome** to set it as your default browser.

Getting Started with Google Chrome

Now that you've installed Google Chrome, it's time to dive into the essentials of using the browser. This section will guide you through launching Chrome for the first time, understanding its user interface, and how to set Chrome as your default browser.

Launching Google Chrome for the First Time

Once Google Chrome is installed on your device, launching it for the first time is simple, and it only takes a few steps depending on the platform you're using.

On Windows

1. **Locate the Chrome Icon**:
   - After installation, Google Chrome may automatically add a shortcut to your desktop. If it's there, double-click the Chrome icon.
   - If it's not on your desktop, you can find it in the Start menu. Click the **Start button** (or press the Windows key) and search for "Google Chrome." Once located, click on the Chrome icon to launch the browser.

2. **First-Time Setup**:
   - When Chrome launches for the first time, it may ask if you want to make Chrome your default browser and whether you want to sign in with your Google account. You can choose to skip or proceed with this setup depending on your preference.

     ○ You may also be asked to import
bookmarks, history, and settings
from another browser.

On macOS

1. **Open Finder**:
     - ○ After installation, Chrome can be
       launched from the **Applications**
       folder. Open Finder, click
       Applications, and find the Google
       Chrome icon.
2. **Launch Chrome**:
     - ○ Double-click the Chrome icon to
       open the browser.
     - ○ For quick access, drag the Chrome
       icon to your dock so you can open
       it easily in the future.
3. **Initial Setup**:
     - ○ The first time you open Chrome,
       macOS will prompt you to confirm
       that you want to open the
       application (since it was
       downloaded from the internet).
       Click **Open** to proceed.

o   Similar to Windows, Chrome may ask if you'd like to make it your default browser and sign in with a Google account.

On Android

1. **Find the Chrome App**:
    o   After installation, you can find Chrome in your app drawer. Open the app drawer by swiping up from the home screen or tapping the app drawer icon.
2. **Launch Chrome**:
    o   Tap the Chrome icon to open it.
    o   If this is your first time launching Chrome, the browser will ask if you want to make Chrome your default web browser. You can also sign in with your Google account to sync your bookmarks and browsing history across devices.

On iOS (iPhone/iPad)

1. **Find Chrome in Your Apps**:
    - After installing, find the Chrome app on your home screen. It will appear like any other app.
2. **Launch Chrome**:
    - Tap the Chrome icon to open the browser.
    - Chrome will ask if you want to sign in to your Google account and sync your settings across devices. You can choose to do so or skip this step for now.

Understanding the Chrome Interface (Tabs, Address Bar, Menu)

One of the reasons Chrome is so popular is due to its simple and intuitive interface. Once you open the browser, understanding its layout will help you navigate websites, manage tabs, and use essential features efficiently. Let's break down the key components of Chrome's interface.

1. Tabs

Tabs allow you to have multiple web pages open in the same browser window, making it easy to switch between websites without closing one to access another.

- **Opening New Tabs**:
  - To open a new tab, click the small "+" icon at the top of the Chrome window (next to the last open tab).
  - Alternatively, you can use the keyboard shortcut **Ctrl + T** (Windows) or **Cmd + T** (Mac).
- **Switching Between Tabs**:
  - Each tab appears at the top of the Chrome window. Simply click on a tab to view its contents.
- **Closing Tabs**:
  - To close a tab, click the small "X" on the right side of the tab, or use the shortcut **Ctrl + W** (Windows) or **Cmd + W** (Mac).
- **Rearranging Tabs**:

- ○ You can drag and drop tabs to reorder them.
- **Pinned Tabs**:
  - ○ Chrome allows you to "pin" frequently used tabs. To pin a tab, right-click on it and choose **Pin Tab**. Pinned tabs stay on the far left and take up less space, ensuring they are always within easy reach.

2. Address Bar (Omnibox)

The address bar, also known as the **Omnibox**, is a powerful feature that doubles as a URL input field and a search bar.

- **Entering a URL**:
  - ○ You can type the URL of a website directly into the address bar and press **Enter**. For example, typing www.google.com and hitting Enter will take you to Google's homepage.
- **Searching from the Address Bar**:

- You can also use the address bar to perform a Google search. Simply type in your search query (e.g., "best restaurants near me") and press Enter.
- **Autocomplete and Suggestions**:
  - As you type in the address bar, Chrome will automatically suggest websites based on your browsing history, bookmarks, and commonly visited sites. You can click on one of these suggestions to go directly to that page.
- **Website Information and Security**:
  - To the left of the URL, you'll see a small icon (usually a padlock). This icon indicates the security status of the website:
    - **Padlock**: The site is secure and uses encryption.
    - **Not Secure**: The site does not use encryption, and any information you enter (like passwords) could be exposed.

3. Menu (Settings and Tools)

In the upper-right corner of the Chrome window, you'll see a three-dot icon. This is the **Menu**, which gives you access to Chrome's settings and other tools.

- **Opening the Menu**:
  - ○ Click the three dots to reveal a dropdown menu with various options. Here are some of the most commonly used options:
- **New Tab, New Window, and Incognito Mode**:
  - ○ The first few options allow you to open new tabs, open a new browser window, or browse in **Incognito Mode** (a private browsing mode where your history and cookies aren't saved).
- **History**:
  - ○ Clicking **History** will show a list of recently visited websites. From here, you can reopen closed tabs or manage your browsing history.

- **Downloads**:
    - ○ In this section, you can view files you've downloaded from the web.
- **Bookmarks**:
    - ○ If you've bookmarked any websites, you can access them quickly from the **Bookmarks** section. You can also manage your bookmarks by adding new ones or organising them into folders.
- **Settings**:
    - ○ Clicking on **Settings** opens Chrome's main configuration options. From here, you can adjust everything from your homepage to privacy settings.

Setting Chrome as Your Default Browser

Making Google Chrome your default browser ensures that all web links you click on (from emails, files, or other apps) will automatically

open in Chrome. Here's how to set Chrome as
your default browser on various platforms.

On Windows

1. **Open Chrome**:
   o Open Google Chrome and click the
     three dots in the top-right corner to
     open the menu.
2. **Access Settings**:
   o From the dropdown menu, click
     Settings.
3. **Set as Default**:
   o Scroll down to the section labelled
     Default Browser.
   o Click the **Make Default** button.
4. **Confirm in Windows Settings**:
   o Windows will open the **Default
     Apps** settings window. In the **Web
     Browser** section, select **Google
     Chrome** from the list of available
     browsers.

On macOS

1. **Open Chrome**:
   - Launch Chrome, and click the three dots in the top-right corner to access the menu.
2. **Go to Settings**:
   - In the dropdown menu, select **Settings**.
3. **Make Default**:
   - Scroll to the **Default Browser** section and click **Make Google Chrome the default browser**.
4. **Confirm on macOS**:
   - If prompted by macOS, confirm your choice by selecting **Use Chrome** as the default option.

On Android

1. **Open Settings**:
   - Go to your device's **Settings** app.
2. **Navigate to Default Apps**:
   - Scroll down to **Apps** or **App Management**, then tap **Default Apps**.
3. **Set Chrome as Default**:

- Under the **Browser App** section, select **Google Chrome** to make it your default browser.

On iOS (iPhone/iPad)

1. **Open Settings**:
   - Go to the iOS **Settings** app.
2. **Find Chrome**:
   - Scroll down and tap on **Chrome** from the list of installed apps.
3. **Set as Default Browser**:
   - Tap on **Default Browser App**, then select **Chrome** from the options.

Navigating the Web with Google Chrome

Once you're familiar with the basics of Google Chrome, it's time to explore its core functionality: navigating the web. Chrome provides various tools to enhance your browsing experience, from entering URLs and searching the web to managing tabs and bookmarks.

Entering URLs and Searching with Chrome's Omnibox

Google Chrome's **Omnibox** is one of the most versatile and powerful tools in the browser. It serves as both the address bar and a search engine, making it easy to navigate the web without switching between different input fields.

1. Entering URLs in the Omnibox

The Omnibox allows you to directly enter the URL (Uniform Resource Locator) of a website to visit it.

- **How to Enter a URL**:
  - Simply click on the Omnibox at the top of your Chrome window, type the website's address (e.g., www.example.com), and press **Enter** on your keyboard.
- **Auto-complete Suggestions**:
  - As you begin typing, Chrome will offer suggestions based on your browsing history, bookmarks, and popular websites. These suggestions allow you to quickly access websites without typing the full URL.
- **Secure Connections (HTTPS)**:

- Chrome displays a padlock icon in the Omnibox to indicate that the website you are visiting uses HTTPS, a secure protocol that encrypts your data. Always look for this padlock when entering sensitive information, like passwords or payment details.

2. Searching the Web Using the Omnibox

The Omnibox also functions as a search bar, allowing you to search the web without needing to visit a search engine's homepage.

- **How to Perform a Search**:
  - Instead of typing a URL, you can simply enter a search query (e.g., "best Italian restaurants near me") directly into the Omnibox and press **Enter**.
- **Google Search Integration**:
  - By default, Chrome uses Google Search for all queries entered in the Omnibox. However, you can

change the default search engine
(such as Bing or DuckDuckGo)
through Chrome's settings.

- **Instant Suggestions**:
  - As you type, Chrome will provide
    instant suggestions, including
    frequently searched terms, websites,
    or even relevant answers to your
    question. These suggestions help
    speed up your browsing experience
    by providing quick access to
    information.
- **Search Shortcuts**:
  - You can also use shortcuts for faster
    navigation. For instance, typing
    "weather" followed by a city name
    (e.g., "weather New York") directly
    in the Omnibox will show the
    current weather for that location
    without having to visit a separate
    website.

Understanding Browser Tabs and Tab Management

Chrome's tabbed browsing feature allows you to open multiple websites simultaneously within the same browser window. Effective tab management is key to maximising productivity and keeping your browsing experience organised.

1. Opening New Tabs

Tabs let you keep multiple web pages open at once, so you can easily switch between them without closing anything.

- **How to Open a New Tab**:
    - To open a new tab, click the "+" icon next to your current tabs at the top of the Chrome window.
    - Alternatively, use the keyboard shortcut **Ctrl + T** (Windows) or **Cmd + T** (Mac) to quickly open a new tab.
- **Opening Links in New Tabs**:

○ If you're on a webpage and want to open a link in a new tab without navigating away from the current page, right-click on the link and select **"Open Link in New Tab"**.

○ On mobile, press and hold the link, then select the same option.

2. Switching Between Tabs

When you have multiple tabs open, switching between them is simple.

- **Click to Switch**:
    ○ Each open tab is displayed at the top of your browser window. Click on any tab to bring it to the front and view its contents.
- **Keyboard Shortcuts**:
    ○ You can switch between tabs quickly using keyboard shortcuts:
        ■ **Ctrl + Tab** (Windows) or **Cmd + Option + Right Arrow** (Mac) will move to the next tab.

- **Ctrl + Shift + Tab**
  (Windows) or **Cmd +
  Option + Left Arrow** (Mac)
  will move to the previous tab.

3. Closing Tabs

When you're finished with a web page, you can close the tab to free up space and reduce clutter.

- **How to Close a Tab**:
  - Click the small **"X"** icon on the tab you want to close. You can also use the keyboard shortcut **Ctrl + W** (Windows) or **Cmd + W** (Mac) to close the current tab.

4. Reopening Closed Tabs

If you accidentally close a tab, Chrome allows you to reopen it quickly.

- **Reopen Last Closed Tab**:
  - Use the shortcut **Ctrl + Shift + T** (Windows) or **Cmd + Shift + T**

(Mac) to reopen the most recently closed tab.

- **History Menu**:
  - ○ Alternatively, you can click the **three-dot menu** (top-right corner), navigate to **History**, and see a list of recently closed tabs.

5. Managing Multiple Tabs

As you open more tabs, it can become harder to keep track of them. Chrome offers several features to help you stay organised.

- **Rearranging Tabs**:
  - ○ You can drag and drop tabs to rearrange their order. This is useful if you have several tabs open and want to prioritise certain websites.
- **Pinning Tabs**:
  - ○ You can pin important tabs (such as your email or calendar) so they stay at the front of your tab list. Right-click on a tab and select **Pin Tab**. Pinned tabs are smaller and

are always placed on the left side of the tab bar.

- **Tab Groups**:
  - ○ Chrome allows you to group related tabs together. Right-click a tab and select **Add to New Group**. You can name the group and assign a colour, which helps visually organise your open tabs.

How to Bookmark Your Favourite Sites

Bookmarks are a great way to save your favourite websites for easy access. Chrome's bookmarking system allows you to store, organise, and access frequently visited pages with just a click.

1. Creating a Bookmark

To create a bookmark, simply save the URL of the website you want to revisit in the future.

- **Click the Star Icon**:
  - While on the webpage you want to bookmark, click the **star** icon located on the far right of the Omnibox.
- **Choose a Folder**:
  - After clicking the star icon, a dialog box will appear. You can name your bookmark and choose where to save it, such as the **Bookmarks Bar** or a custom folder.
- **Using Keyboard Shortcuts**:
  - You can also use the shortcut **Ctrl + D** (Windows) or **Cmd + D** (Mac) to quickly bookmark a page.

2. Accessing Bookmarked Pages

Your bookmarks are easily accessible from Chrome's **Bookmarks Bar** or the **Bookmarks Menu**.

- **Bookmarks Bar**:
  - The Bookmarks Bar appears just below the Omnibox and displays

your most commonly used
bookmarks. You can toggle the
Bookmarks Bar on or off by
pressing **Ctrl + Shift + B**
(Windows) or **Cmd + Shift + B**
(Mac).

- **Bookmarks Menu**:
  - You can also access all your
    bookmarks by clicking the
    three-dot menu and navigating to
    **Bookmarks > Bookmark
    Manager**. From here, you can view,
    edit, and organise all your saved
    bookmarks.

3. Organising Your Bookmarks

If you have many bookmarks, organising them
into folders can make it easier to find what
you're looking for.

- **Create Folders**:
  - Open the **Bookmark Manager** (via
    the menu or by pressing **Ctrl +
    Shift + O**), then click **Organise >**

> **Add Folder** to create a new folder. You can drag and drop bookmarks into these folders to keep things organised.

- **Edit or Delete Bookmarks**:
  - To edit or delete a bookmark, open the Bookmark Manager, right-click on the bookmark, and choose **Edit** or **Delete**.

Using Chrome's History to Revisit Pages

Google Chrome automatically keeps a record of every website you visit. This is helpful if you want to revisit a page but can't remember the URL or if you accidentally close a tab.

1. Viewing Your Browsing History

Chrome's **History** feature stores a chronological list of websites you've visited, making it easy to find and revisit them.

- **Access History**:
  - ○ To access your browsing history, click the **three-dot menu** in the top-right corner of Chrome, then select **History** > **History**.
  - ○ You can also use the shortcut **Ctrl + H** (Windows) or **Cmd + Y** (Mac) to open the History page directly.
- **Revisiting Pages**:
  - ○ Once on the History page, you'll see a list of recently visited websites. Click on any link to open that page again.

2. Searching Your History

If you're looking for a specific page but don't remember when you visited it, you can search your browsing history.

- **Search Bar**:
  - ○ At the top of the History page, you'll find a search bar. Enter any keyword or phrase related to the page you're trying to find (such as

the site's name or part of the URL), and Chrome will show all relevant results.

3. Clearing Your History

If you want to remove some or all of your browsing history for privacy reasons, Chrome allows you to do so.

- **How to Clear History**:
    - To clear your browsing history, click **Clear Browsing Data** from the History page. You can choose to clear specific time ranges (e.g., last hour, last 24 hours, all time) and specify which data to delete (browsing history, cookies, cached files, etc.).

Customising Google Chrome

One of Google Chrome's greatest strengths is its ability to be customised according to your preferences. Whether you want to change its appearance, enhance its functionality with extensions, or manage multiple users through profiles, Chrome gives you a variety of options to make your browsing experience more personalised and efficient.

Changing Chrome's Appearance (Themes, Fonts, and Layout)

Google Chrome allows you to change its visual appearance to suit your personal taste. From altering the browser's theme to customise the font size and style, Chrome offers plenty of options to enhance your browsing experience.

1. Applying Themes in Chrome

Themes change the overall look and feel of Chrome's interface, including the background, tab bar, and Omnibox. Chrome themes can be light or dark, colourful or minimalistic, and come in a wide variety of designs.

- **How to Access Chrome Themes**:
    - Click the **three-dot menu** (top-right corner of the browser) and navigate to **Settings** > **Appearance** > **Theme**. This will direct you to the **Chrome Web Store**, where you can browse available themes.
- **Installing a Theme**:
    - In the Chrome Web Store, you can search for a theme that suits your preferences. Once you find one, click on it, then select **Add to Chrome**. The theme will be applied

immediately, changing the colour
and background of your browser.

- **Removing or Resetting a Theme**:
  - If you want to revert to Chrome's
    default appearance or try a new
    theme, go back to **Settings** >
    Appearance and select **Reset to
    Default** to remove the current
    theme.

2. Customising Fonts in Chrome

Chrome also allows you to adjust the font style
and size for better readability. This is especially
useful if you frequently visit websites with small
text or if you want to enhance the visual appeal
of the content you're reading.

- **How to Change Font Settings**:
  - Navigate to **Settings** > **Appearance**
    > **Customise Fonts**. Here, you can
    adjust the **font size** (default, small,
    or large) and even pick specific font
    types for standard text, serif fonts,
    and monospace fonts.

- **Advanced Font Customization**:
  - For more control over font styles, you can manually set the minimum font size, or choose from a variety of available fonts like Arial, Times New Roman, or Verdana.

3. Adjusting Page Layout (Zoom and Page Scaling)

Chrome provides layout customization options like zooming in and out on web pages, which can make content easier to read or fit more information on the screen.

- **Page Zoom**:
  - To zoom in or out, click the **three-dot menu**, and under **Zoom**, use the plus (+) or minus (-) buttons to adjust the zoom level. You can also use the keyboard shortcuts **Ctrl + Plus** (zoom in) or **Ctrl + Minus** (zoom out) on Windows, or **Cmd + Plus** / **Cmd + Minus** on Mac.
- **Full-Screen Mode**:

○ For a distraction-free browsing experience, press **F11** (Windows) or **Cmd + Ctrl + F** (Mac) to enter **Full-Screen Mode**, where the entire screen is dedicated to the current webpage.

Setting Up and Managing Extensions

Extensions are small software programs that add new features to Chrome, making it more powerful and tailored to your specific needs. With extensions, you can block ads, manage your passwords, integrate with other apps, and more.

1. How to Find and Install Extensions

Extensions can be found in the **Chrome Web Store**, where they are categorised based on functionality, such as productivity, security, or entertainment.

- **Accessing the Chrome Web Store**:
  - To find extensions, click the **three-dot menu**, then go to **More Tools** > **Extensions**. At the bottom of the page, click **Get more extensions** to be redirected to the Chrome Web Store.
- **Installing Extensions**:
  - Once you find an extension you want to add, click **Add to Chrome**. You may be prompted to give the extension certain permissions, such as access to your browsing data. After you approve, the extension will be installed and its icon will appear next to the Omnibox.
- **Popular Extensions**:
  - Some of the most commonly used extensions include:
    - **AdBlock**: Blocks intrusive ads on websites.
    - **Grammarly**: Check your spelling and grammar as you type.

- **LastPass**: Manages your passwords securely.
- **Google Translate**: Instantly translates web pages.
- **Evernote Web Clipper**: Saves web content for later reading.

2. Managing Your Extensions

Once you have installed several extensions, managing them effectively becomes important to ensure your browser runs smoothly.

- **Accessing Installed Extensions**:
  - Go to **Settings** > **Extensions** to see a list of all installed extensions. From here, you can enable, disable, or remove extensions.
- **Disabling Extensions**:
  - If an extension is causing issues or you want to temporarily turn it off, click the toggle switch next to the extension name to disable it. This

will prevent it from running without uninstalling it.

- **Removing Extensions**:
  - ○ If you no longer need an extension, click the **Remove** button on the **Extensions** page to uninstall it completely.

3. Extension Settings and Permissions

Some extensions allow for customization, such as adjusting settings or setting up custom rules for how the extension behaves.

- **Customising Extension Settings**:
  - ○ Many extensions offer their own settings page. You can access these by clicking on the extension icon next to the Omnibox and selecting **Options** or **Settings**.
- **Managing Extension Permissions**:
  - ○ Extensions often request permissions, like access to your browsing history or the ability to change site data. You can review

and adjust these permissions on the **Extensions** page by clicking **Details** under each extension and modifying what the extension has access to.

Personalising Your Startup Page and Default Search Engine

Customising what happens when you first open Chrome, as well as which search engine you use, can significantly enhance your browsing efficiency.

1. Setting Your Startup Page

Chrome allows you to decide what you see when you first open the browser. You can choose between a blank new tab page, your most visited sites, or a custom set of pages.

- **Choosing a Startup Option**:
    - Navigate to **Settings** > **On startup**. Here, you can choose from:

- **Open the New Tab page**: Chrome will display a blank new tab with shortcuts to your most frequently visited websites.
- **Continue where you left off**: Chrome will open all the tabs you had open when you last closed the browser.
- **Open a specific page or set of pages**: You can set one or more specific websites (e.g., news sites, your email, or your calendar) to automatically open whenever you start Chrome.

- **Adding or Removing Startup Pages**:
  - If you choose the "specific pages" option, click **Add a new page** to enter the URL of the website you want to open. You can also remove pages from the list by clicking **Remove** next to the page URL.

2. Setting Your Default Search Engine

By default, Chrome uses **Google Search**, but you can customise the browser to use any search engine you prefer.

- **Changing the Default Search Engine**:
    - Go to **Settings** > **Search engine**. In the **Search engine used in the address bar** dropdown, select your preferred search engine (such as **Bing**, **Yahoo!**, or **DuckDuckGo**).
- **Adding a Custom Search Engine**:
    - If your preferred search engine is not listed, click **Manage search engines and site search**. Here, you can add a new search engine by entering its name, keyword, and URL.

Chrome Profiles: Managing Multiple Users and Syncing Across Devices

If multiple people use the same computer or you want to keep your work and personal browsing separate, Chrome's profile feature is ideal. Profiles allow each user to have their own customised Chrome environment, with separate settings, extensions, bookmarks, and saved passwords. Additionally, profiles can sync across multiple devices for seamless browsing.

1. Creating and Managing Chrome Profiles

Creating a separate Chrome profile allows you to keep your browsing data, such as history, passwords, and bookmarks, separate from other users.

- **Creating a New Profile**:
    - Click the **profile icon** in the top-right corner of Chrome, then click **Add**. Follow the prompts to create a new profile, giving it a name and choosing a theme colour or avatar.
- **Switching Between Profiles**:

- Once multiple profiles are set up, you can switch between them by clicking the **profile icon** and selecting the desired profile from the dropdown menu.
- **Managing Profiles**:
  - To manage profiles, go to **Settings > You and Google > Profiles**. From here, you can edit or delete profiles, or add new ones.

2. Syncing Across Devices

Chrome's **Sync** feature allows you to synchronise your browsing data across all your devices. This means you can access your bookmarks, saved passwords, and browsing history from your phone, tablet, and desktop seamlessly.

- **Enabling Sync**:
  - To enable sync, you must sign in to Chrome with your **Google Account**. Go to **Settings > You and Google > Sync and Google**

services. Toggle the **Sync** switch to on, then choose what you want to sync, such as bookmarks, history, passwords, and extensions.

- **Benefits of Syncing**:
  - Syncing makes it easy to switch between devices while maintaining access to all your personal settings. For example, if you bookmark a website on your computer, it will be available on your smartphone automatically.

Using Chrome Features Effectively

Google Chrome provides a wide array of features that enhance your browsing experience, from saving personal information for quick autofill to private browsing options and managing bookmarks efficiently. Mastering these tools will allow you to browse the web with ease, keep track of important sites, and protect your privacy when needed.

Chrome Autofill: Saving Passwords, Addresses, and Payment Methods

Autofill is one of Chrome's most convenient features, enabling you to save and automatically fill in personal details like passwords, addresses, and payment methods on websites you frequently visit. This feature helps save time and ensures smooth and quick form-filling across the web.

1. Saving Passwords with Chrome Autofill

Chrome can securely save your passwords for the websites you log into. Each time you enter a new password, Chrome offers to save it so you can log in automatically the next time.

- **How to Save Passwords**:
    - When you log into a website for the first time, Chrome will display a prompt asking if you want to save the password. Click **Save** to store it. If you don't want to save it, you can choose **Never** or **Not Now**.
- **Managing Saved Passwords**:
    - To manage your saved passwords, go to **Settings** > **Autofill** >

Passwords. Here, you'll see a list of websites with saved passwords. You can view, delete, or update any saved password. Additionally, you can enable or disable the **Auto Sign-In** feature, which automatically logs you into sites without prompting you.

- **Security for Saved Passwords**:
  - Chrome stores your passwords securely, and you can require authentication (like your computer's password or fingerprint) before viewing saved passwords. You can also use Chrome's built-in password check tool to identify weak or compromised passwords and update them for enhanced security.

2. Storing and Managing Addresses

Chrome's Autofill feature can also save your personal information, such as home or work addresses, making it easy to complete forms when shopping online or registering for events.

- **Saving Addresses**:
  - ○ When you fill out a form that requires your address, Chrome will prompt you to save the information. Once saved, Chrome can automatically fill in your address the next time it's required on a website.
- **Managing Saved Addresses**:
  - ○ Go to **Settings** > **Autofill** > **Addresses and more** to manage your saved addresses. You can add, edit, or delete addresses, as well as choose whether Chrome should offer to save new addresses.

3. Storing Payment Methods

For online shopping and transactions, Chrome's Autofill feature can store your credit or debit card details, making the checkout process faster and easier.

- **Saving Payment Methods**:
  - When you enter your credit card information on a website, Chrome will ask if you'd like to save the payment method for future use. If you agree, it will store the card details and automatically fill them the next time you make a purchase.
- **Managing Payment Methods**:
  - Go to **Settings** > **Autofill** > **Payment methods** to manage your stored cards. You can view, edit, or remove payment methods, as well as decide whether to allow Chrome to prompt you to save new cards. Payment information is stored securely, and Chrome requires confirmation before any auto filled data is used.

Using Incognito Mode for Private Browsing

Incognito Mode is Chrome's private browsing feature that prevents your browsing history, cookies, and site data from being saved. It's ideal when you want to browse without leaving any traces on your device, such as when shopping for a gift on a shared computer or researching sensitive topics.

1. What Happens in Incognito Mode

When you use Incognito Mode, Chrome does not save any information about the websites you visit, the files you download, or the forms you fill out. It also prevents cookies and site data from being saved, meaning websites won't remember your visit after you close the Incognito window.

- **What Incognito Does**:
  - Browsing history is not saved.
  - Cookies and site data are cleared when you close the window.
  - Autofill information is not saved, unless manually entered.
- **What Incognito Doesn't Do**:

○ It doesn't make you anonymous
online. Websites, your internet
service provider (ISP), or network
administrators can still track your
activity.
○ It doesn't prevent malware or
viruses from being downloaded.

2. How to Open Incognito Mode

To open an Incognito window:

- Click the **three-dot menu** in the top-right
corner of Chrome.
- Select **New Incognito Window** from the
dropdown menu.
- A new window with a dark theme and a
message explaining the features of
Incognito Mode will appear.

Alternatively, you can use the keyboard shortcut
Ctrl + Shift + N on Windows or **Cmd + Shift +
N** on Mac to open an Incognito window.

3. Managing Incognito Sessions

While in Incognito Mode, you can open multiple tabs, and Chrome will treat all of them as part of the same Incognito session. When you're done, simply close the Incognito window, and all session data, including history and cookies, will be erased.

- **Switching Between Regular and Incognito Windows**:
  - ○ You can have both regular and Incognito windows open at the same time. The Incognito window will remain private, while the regular window will store data as usual.

How to Use Chrome's Downloads Manager

Chrome's Downloads Manager helps you keep track of the files you download from the internet, ensuring that you can easily locate, pause, or resume downloads as needed.

1. Accessing the Downloads Manager

The Downloads Manager keeps a record of all the files you've downloaded via Chrome.

- **How to Open Downloads Manager**:
  - To access the Downloads Manager, click the **three-dot menu** and select **Downloads**, or use the keyboard shortcut **Ctrl + J** (Windows) or **Cmd + J** (Mac).
- **Viewing Download History**:
  - The Downloads page displays a list of your recent downloads, including the file name, download location, and download status. If you haven't changed your settings, downloads are usually saved to the **Downloads** folder on your computer.

2. Managing Downloads

The Downloads Manager gives you control over ongoing and completed downloads.

- **Pausing and Resuming Downloads**:

- If you're downloading a large file and need to temporarily halt the process, click **Pause** next to the file in the Downloads Manager. When you're ready to continue, click **Resume**.
- **Opening or Locating Downloaded Files**:
  - Once a download is complete, you can open the file directly from the Downloads Manager by clicking on its name. To locate the file on your computer, click **Show in folder** (Windows) or **Show in Finder** (Mac).

3. Deleting and Clearing Downloads

To free up space or remove clutter, you can delete downloaded files or clear your download history.

- **Removing Download History**:
  - In the Downloads Manager, click **Remove from list** next to any completed download to remove it

from the list without deleting the file itself.

- **Deleting Downloaded Files**:
    - ○ If you want to delete the downloaded file from your computer, go to the file's location and manually delete it.

Setting Up and Managing Chrome Bookmarks and Folders

Bookmarks are an essential tool for keeping track of your favourite websites, allowing you to revisit important pages with just a click. Chrome makes it easy to create and organise bookmarks in folders for efficient navigation.

1. Adding Bookmarks

Creating a bookmark in Chrome is simple and can be done from any webpage.

- **How to Bookmark a Page**:

- ○ While on a webpage you want to save, click the **star icon** in the Omnibox (address bar). You can also use the keyboard shortcut **Ctrl + D** (Windows) or **Cmd + D** (Mac) to instantly bookmark the page.
- **Choosing Where to Save a Bookmark**:
  - ○ When you create a bookmark, Chrome will ask you to choose a location for it. By default, bookmarks are saved in the **Bookmarks bar**, but you can also create new folders or choose other existing ones to keep your bookmarks organised.

2. Organising Bookmarks with Folders

As you collect more bookmarks, organising them into folders helps you quickly find the sites you need.

- **Creating Bookmark Folders**:
  - ○ To create a new folder, click **Bookmarks** from the **three-dot**

menu and select **Bookmark Manager**. Here, you can right-click or tap **Organise**, then select **Add Folder**. Give the folder a name (e.g., "Work," "Recipes," "Tech News") and drag bookmarks into the folder to group them.

- **Moving Bookmarks**:
  - You can move bookmarks between folders by dragging and dropping them in the **Bookmark Manager** or by selecting **Edit** from the right-click menu.

3. Using the Bookmarks Bar

The **Bookmarks bar** is a quick-access toolbar that appears below the Omnibox and provides instant access to your most frequently used bookmarks.

- **Enabling the Bookmarks Bar**:
  - To show or hide the Bookmarks bar, press **Ctrl + Shift + B** (Windows) or **Cmd + Shift + B** (Mac). You can

also enable it via **Settings >
Appearance > Show Bookmarks
Bar**.

- **Managing Bookmarks from the
Bookmarks Bar**:
  - ○ You can drag bookmarks onto the
bar for quick access or drag them
into folders to organise them
further.

Chrome Security and Privacy

In the digital age, security and privacy are crucial concerns for internet users. Google Chrome, being one of the most widely used browsers, comes equipped with a range of built-in security features and privacy controls that help protect users from threats such as malware, phishing, and tracking by websites. Learning how to manage these tools can help you keep your browsing sessions secure and protect your personal information.

Understanding Chrome's Built-in Security Features

Google Chrome takes a proactive approach to user security, implementing features designed to safeguard your data and browsing activity from malicious threats.

1. Safe Browsing Protection

Chrome's Safe Browsing feature is a robust system that protects you from dangerous websites and downloads.

- **How Safe Browsing Works**:
  - Safe Browsing identifies and warns you when you attempt to visit potentially harmful sites, such as phishing pages that try to steal your personal information or sites that distribute malware. If Chrome detects a suspicious website, it will display a full-page warning that advises you not to proceed.
- **Enhanced Protection**:
  - Chrome offers an **Enhanced Safe Browsing** mode that provides additional protection by sharing

real-time data with Google about potentially dangerous websites or suspicious activity. You can enable it in **Settings** > **Privacy and security** > **Safe Browsing** > **Enhanced Protection**. This setting improves protection against phishing, malware, and other online threats.

2. Sandboxing

One of Chrome's key security innovations is **sandboxing**, which isolates each browser tab or web app from others. This ensures that if one tab becomes compromised by malware or malicious code, the rest of the browser remains unaffected.

- **How Sandboxing Works**:
  - Every tab or extension you open in Chrome runs in a separate process, making it difficult for malicious software to spread across tabs or access your files. If a threat is detected, Chrome shuts down the

affected tab without risking your other tabs or the entire browser.

3. Automatic Updates

Chrome regularly receives security updates that automatically protect against the latest threats and vulnerabilities.

- **Keeping Chrome Up-to-Date**:
  - Chrome checks for updates automatically and applies them in the background. If an update requires a browser restart, Chrome will notify you. It's essential to keep your browser updated to benefit from the latest security enhancements.

4. Built-in Password Manager and Security Checkup

Chrome has a built-in password manager that securely stores your passwords, but it goes beyond that by offering a **Password Checkup** feature that alerts you if any of your saved passwords have been exposed in a data breach.

- **Using Password Checkup**:
    - To check if any of your passwords have been compromised, go to **Settings** > **Autofill** > **Passwords**, then click **Check passwords**. Chrome will scan your saved passwords and flag any that are weak, reused, or compromised, allowing you to update them for better security.

Managing Cookies and Site Permissions

Cookies and site permissions control how websites interact with your browser and your data. By managing these settings, you can balance the convenience of customised web experiences with protecting your privacy.

1. What Are Cookies?

Cookies are small text files stored on your device by websites you visit. They remember your login credentials, preferences, and browsing activity, making it easier to navigate websites without re-entering information. However, cookies can also be used to track your activity across multiple sites for targeted advertising.

- **First-Party vs. Third-Party Cookies**:
  - **First-party cookies** are created by the website you're visiting and usually improve the user experience by remembering your preferences.
  - **Third-party cookies** are created by external advertisers or analytics services embedded on the website. These cookies track your activity across multiple websites and are often used for targeted ads.

2. How to Manage Cookies

Chrome provides several options for managing cookies, from blocking them entirely to allowing only certain types.

- **Blocking Third-Party Cookies**:
  - ○ You can block third-party cookies without affecting first-party cookies, which allows you to maintain convenience while reducing tracking. To do this, go to **Settings** > **Privacy and security** > **Cookies and other site data**, then select **Block third-party cookies**.
- **Clearing Cookies**:
  - ○ If you want to delete cookies for privacy reasons or to troubleshoot website issues, you can clear them by going to **Settings** > **Privacy and security** > **Clear browsing data**. Here, you can choose to delete cookies from the last hour, day, week, or all time.

3. Managing Site Permissions

Different websites may request access to various features of your device, such as your camera, microphone, location, or notifications. Chrome allows you to manage these permissions, ensuring you have control over how websites interact with your data.

- **How to Manage Site Permissions**:
  - Go to **Settings** > **Privacy and security** > **Site Settings**. Here, you can control which sites are allowed to access your location, camera, microphone, notifications, JavaScript, and more. For example, you can block a website from accessing your camera but still allow it to send notifications.
- **Customising Permissions for Individual Sites**:
  - When visiting a website, you can customise its permissions by clicking the **lock icon** to the left of the URL in the address bar. This menu allows you to quickly allow

or block specific permissions for that site.

Blocking Pop-ups and Managing Ads

Pop-ups and intrusive ads can disrupt your browsing experience and, in some cases, pose security risks. Chrome offers tools to block unwanted pop-ups and manage ads more effectively.

1. Blocking Pop-ups

Chrome's default setting blocks most pop-ups, but some sites may still attempt to open them. Pop-ups can be used for legitimate purposes (such as login windows or online chats) or for more disruptive activities (like ads or phishing attempts).

- **How to Block Pop-ups**:
    - To control pop-ups, go to **Settings > Privacy and security > Site**

Settings > **Pop-ups and redirects**.
You can block all pop-ups or allow
them only for specific sites you
trust.

2. Managing Ads

Chrome's ad-blocking features help reduce the
number of intrusive or deceptive ads that can
interfere with your browsing. The browser also
works to prevent ads that may contain malware
or inappropriate content.

- **How to Control Ads**:
  - Chrome automatically blocks ads
    that violate the **Better Ads
    Standards** by default. You can
    adjust ad settings by going to
    **Settings > Privacy and security >
    Site Settings > Ads**. You can
    choose to block ads on all sites or
    allow them only on certain
    websites.

How to Clear Browsing Data (Cache, Cookies, History)

Clearing your browsing data is essential for protecting your privacy, freeing up storage, and improving browser performance. Chrome allows you to delete various types of browsing data, including your cache, cookies, and browsing history.

1. What Browsing Data Can Be Cleared?

When you clear your browsing data in Chrome, you can choose which types of data to delete:

- **Browsing history**: A list of all the websites you've visited.
- **Cookies and other site data**: Stored data that websites use to remember you and your preferences.
- **Cached images and files**: Temporary files stored to load websites faster on repeat visits.
- **Passwords and Autofill data**: Saved login credentials and form entries.

2. How to Clear Browsing Data

To clear your browsing data in Chrome:

1. Click the **three-dot menu** in the top-right corner of Chrome and select **Settings**.
2. Go to **Privacy and security** > **Clear browsing data**.
3. In the pop-up window, choose which types of data you want to delete and select a time range (e.g., last hour, last 24 hours, all time).
4. Click **Clear data** to remove the selected information.

3. Advanced Data Clearing Options

Chrome also provides advanced options for managing your data:

- **Time Range**: You can clear data from the last hour, day, week, month, or all time.
- **Specific Site Data**: To clear data from a particular site, go to **Settings** > **Privacy and security** > **Site Settings** > **View permissions and data stored across**

sites. Here, you can remove cookies and data for individual websites without affecting others.

4. Why Clear Browsing Data?

Clearing browsing data can improve your browsing experience in several ways:

- **Protect Your Privacy**: By clearing cookies and browsing history, you prevent other users of your device from seeing your online activity.
- **Improve Browser Performance**: Large amounts of cached data can slow down Chrome over time. Clearing the cache can help improve speed and performance.
- **Fix Website Errors**: Sometimes websites may not load correctly due to outdated cookies or cached files. Clearing your browsing data can resolve these issues.

Working with Extensions in Google Chrome

Google Chrome's versatility extends beyond its basic browsing capabilities through the use of extensions. These small software programs integrate directly into the browser, enhancing functionality, productivity, security, and entertainment. Understanding how to install, manage, and utilise extensions effectively can significantly personalise your browsing experience.

What Are Chrome Extensions?

Chrome extensions are mini-programs that add new features and functionalities to your Chrome browser. They are designed to customise your browsing experience, improve productivity, enhance security, and even modify how websites behave.

1. Types of Chrome Extensions

Extensions can serve a wide range of purposes, including:

- **Productivity**: Tools that help you manage tasks, organise information, or automate repetitive actions.
- **Security**: Enhancements that protect your privacy, block ads, or guard against malicious websites.
- **Entertainment**: Add-ons that provide music, games, or other forms of online entertainment.
- **Customization**: Tools that personalise the appearance and behaviour of websites or the browser itself.

2. How Extensions Work

Extensions typically interact with web pages by modifying their content or behaviour. They can add buttons to the Chrome toolbar, create new menus, modify existing web pages, or provide alerts and notifications.

- **Permissions**: When you install an extension, it may request specific permissions to access your browsing data, tabs, or other information. It's essential to review these permissions before installation to ensure the extension's legitimacy and suitability for your needs.
- **Chrome Web Store**: Extensions are primarily sourced from the Chrome Web Store, which categorises them by type and popularity. Users can browse, search, and install extensions directly from this platform.

Installing and Managing Extensions

Chrome makes it straightforward to install and manage extensions, allowing you to customise your browser with tools that cater to your specific interests and needs.

1. Installing Extensions

To install an extension from the Chrome Web Store:

1. **Navigate to the Chrome Web Store**: Visit the Chrome Web Store using your Chrome browser.
2. **Search or Browse**: Use the search bar to find extensions by name or browse categories such as Productivity, Security, Entertainment, etc.
3. **Choose an Extension**: Click on an extension to view more details, including its description, reviews, and screenshots.
4. **Install**: Click the **Add to Chrome** button. A confirmation dialog may appear asking for permission to add the extension. Click **Add extension** to proceed.

5. **Confirmation**: Once installed, the extension's icon typically appears in the Chrome toolbar, and you may receive a notification confirming its addition.

2. Managing Extensions

Managing extensions allows you to control their behaviour, update settings, or remove them if they are no longer needed or causing issues.

- **Accessing Extensions**:
  - To manage extensions, click on the **three-dot menu** in the top-right corner of Chrome, then go to **More tools > Extensions**. Alternatively, you can type chrome://extensions/ in the address bar and press Enter.
- **Managing Options**:
  - **Enable or Disable**: Toggle the switch next to each extension to enable or disable it.
  - **Remove**: Click the **Remove** button to uninstall an extension completely from your browser.

- ○ **Options**: Some extensions offer additional settings or options that can be accessed by clicking **Details** under the extension in the Extensions page.
- **Updating Extensions**:
  - ○ Extensions are automatically updated by Chrome to ensure they are secure and up-to-date. You can manually check for updates by visiting the Extensions page and clicking **Update** if available.

Popular Extensions for Productivity, Entertainment, and Security

Extensions cater to various user needs, providing tools that range from boosting productivity to enhancing online security and providing entertainment options.

1. Productivity Extensions

- **Grammarly**: Helps improve writing by checking grammar, spelling, and style.
- **Todoist**: A task manager for creating to-do lists and managing tasks.
- **LastPass**: Password manager that securely stores and autofills passwords.
- **Pocket**: Save articles, videos, and web pages to view later, even offline.

2. Security Extensions

- **Adblock Plus**: Blocks intrusive ads and pop-ups, enhancing browsing speed and security.
- **HTTPS Everywhere**: Ensures secure connections by automatically redirecting websites to HTTPS versions where available.
- **Avast Online Security**: Alerts you to suspicious websites and phishing attempts, helping to keep your browsing safe.

3. Entertainment Extensions

- **Honey**: Automatically finds and applies coupon codes when shopping online.
- **YouTube Video Downloader**: Allows you to download YouTube videos for offline viewing.
- **Enhancer for YouTube**: Enhances the YouTube watching experience with features like pop-out player and ad skipping.

4. Customization Extensions

- **Dark Reader**: Inverts website colours to reduce eye strain and improve readability in low-light environments.
- **Stylish**: Customise the appearance of websites with themes and user-created styles.
- **Speed Dial 2**: Replaces the default new tab page with a customizable dashboard for quick access to your favourite sites.

Syncing Chrome Across Devices

Google Chrome's sync feature is one of the most powerful tools for users who operate across multiple devices, whether it be a desktop computer, laptop, smartphone, or tablet. By signing in to Chrome with your Google Account, you can seamlessly sync your browsing data, including bookmarks, history, passwords, and extensions, across all of your devices. This makes it easier to pick up where you left off, access your saved information, and maintain a consistent browsing experience, no matter where you are or what device you're using.

How to Sign In and Sync Chrome with a Google Account

The first step in syncing Chrome across multiple devices is to sign in with your Google Account. Once signed in, Chrome can start syncing your data and preferences to provide a seamless experience across different platforms.

1. Signing in to Chrome

To sign in to Chrome and begin syncing your data, follow these steps:

- **On Desktop (Windows and Mac)**:
    1. Open Google Chrome on your computer.
    2. Click the **Profile icon** in the top-right corner of the browser window (this could be a generic profile picture or a "head-and-shoulders" icon).
    3. Select **Sign in to Chrome** or **Turn on sync** if you are already using a profile.

4. Enter your Google Account email and password.

5. After signing in, you will be prompted to **Turn on sync**. Click **Yes, I'm in** to enable syncing.

- **On Mobile (Android and iOS)**:
  1. Open Google Chrome on your smartphone or tablet.
  2. Tap the **three-dot menu** in the top-right corner (Android) or bottom-right corner (iOS) of the screen.
  3. Tap **Settings** and then **Sign in to Chrome** or **Turn on sync**.
  4. Enter your Google Account credentials and choose **Yes, I'm in** to activate sync.

Once you've signed in on any device, Chrome will immediately begin syncing your browsing data across all devices connected to the same Google Account.

Syncing Bookmarks, History, and Extensions

Chrome syncs a wide range of data between devices, ensuring that your browsing experience is consistent and unified. Here are the main types of data you can sync:

1. Bookmarks

Bookmarks allow you to save web pages that you want to revisit later. Syncing bookmarks ensures that you have access to all your saved sites on every device.

- When syncing is enabled, any changes you make to your bookmarks on one device will automatically update across all other synced devices. For example, if you bookmark a website on your desktop, it will also appear in the bookmarks bar of your Chrome browser on your smartphone or tablet.

2. Browsing History

Your browsing history is a record of the websites you've visited, and with Chrome sync, you can access this history across devices.

- This feature is particularly useful if you need to continue reading an article you started on your laptop while using your smartphone or if you want to search for a website you visited earlier in the day without having to manually re-enter the URL.

3. Extensions

Chrome extensions provide additional functionality to the browser, from productivity tools to entertainment options. Syncing extensions allows you to maintain the same set of tools across multiple devices.

- When you install an extension on one device, Chrome will automatically sync it to your other devices. For example, if you add a password manager extension on your desktop, you will be able to use the same extension on your laptop without needing to install it again.

4. Passwords and Autofill Data

Chrome can store your passwords, payment information, and other autofill data, making it easier to log in to websites or fill out online forms. When sync is enabled, this data is securely shared across all your devices.

- For instance, if you save your login credentials for an online shopping site on your desktop, Chrome will automatically fill in the same details on your smartphone when you visit the site, saving you time and effort.

5. Open Tabs

With Chrome sync, you can see the tabs you have open on other devices. This is perfect for continuing your browsing session when switching from one device to another.

- For example, if you leave multiple tabs open on your work computer, you can easily access them later from your phone or tablet without having to manually reopen each one.

Managing Your Synced Data

Syncing is a powerful tool, but it's also important to manage it properly to ensure that your data is protected and your browsing experience remains smooth. Chrome gives you full control over what data is synced and provides options for adjusting these settings.

1. Customizing Sync Settings

While Chrome syncs a wide range of data by default, you have the option to choose which types of information are synced between devices.

- **On Desktop (Windows and Mac):**

1. Click the **three-dot menu** in the top-right corner of Chrome.
2. Select **Settings**.
3. Under the **You and Google** section, click **Sync and Google services**.
4. Click **Manage what you sync**.
5. You can either choose **Sync everything** or manually select the individual data types you want to sync, such as bookmarks, history, passwords, extensions, and more.

- **On Mobile (Android and iOS):**
  1. Tap the **three-dot menu** in the Chrome app and go to **Settings**.
  2. Tap your **Google Account** at the top.
  3. Tap **Sync**.
  4. From here, you can toggle specific data types on or off, such as bookmarks, history, and passwords.

2. Managing Synced Data from Your Google Account

In addition to managing synced data directly from Chrome, you can also view and manage synced data through your Google Account.

1. Visit **myaccount.google.com**.
2. Under the **Data & privacy** tab, scroll down to the **Things you create and do** section.
3. Click **Manage your Google Chrome sync** to view detailed information about your synced data, such as bookmarks, saved passwords, and browsing history.

3. Encrypting Your Synced Data

Chrome offers advanced security options, including the ability to encrypt your synced data with a passphrase. By default, Chrome encrypted passwords, but you can opt to encrypt all your data for added protection.

- **How to Set Up a Passphrase**:
    1. Go to Chrome **Settings** > **Sync and Google services**.
    2. Click **Encryption options**.

3. Select **Encrypt synced data with your own passphrase** and create a passphrase. This passphrase is required on all your devices to decrypt the data, ensuring that only you have access to your synced information.

4. Managing Sync Conflicts

If you use Chrome on multiple devices, sometimes data conflicts can occur, such as having two different versions of the same bookmark or extension settings. Chrome automatically handles most conflicts, but if you notice discrepancies, you can manually adjust them in the **Sync and Google services** section of your Chrome settings.

5. Turning Off Sync

If you no longer want to sync your data, you can easily turn off the sync feature.

- **On Desktop**:
  1. Open Chrome **Settings**.

2. Click on your **Google Account**.
3. Select **Turn off sync**.

- **On Mobile**:
    1. Open the Chrome app and tap the **three-dot menu**.
    2. Go to **Settings** and tap your Google Account.
    3. Tap **Sync** and toggle it off.

Disabling sync will stop Chrome from sharing your data across devices, but your existing synced data will remain stored in your Google Account unless you choose to delete it.

Chrome Shortcuts and Productivity Tips

Google Chrome is designed with a user-friendly interface that promotes efficient browsing. To enhance productivity and streamline your online activities, mastering keyboard shortcuts and leveraging Chrome's built-in tools is essential. This section will explore various keyboard shortcuts, the Chrome Task Manager, and strategies for managing tabs effectively, including tab groups and pinned tabs.

Keyboard Shortcuts for Faster Browsing

Keyboard shortcuts are a great way to enhance your browsing efficiency, allowing you to navigate quickly through the Chrome interface and perform common actions without relying on your mouse. Here are some of the most useful keyboard shortcuts for both Windows and macOS users:

Common Shortcuts

- **Open a New Tab**:
    - **Windows**: Ctrl + T
    - **Mac**: Command + T
- **Close Current Tab**:
    - **Windows**: Ctrl + W
    - **Mac**: Command + W
- **Reopen Last Closed Tab**:
    - **Windows**: Ctrl + Shift + T
    - **Mac**: Command + Shift + T
- **Switch Between Tabs**:
    - **Next Tab**:
        - **Windows**: Ctrl + Tab or Ctrl + Page Down
        - **Mac**: Command + Option + Right Arrow

- ○ **Previous Tab**:
    - ■ **Windows**: Ctrl + Shift + Tab or Ctrl + Page Up
    - ■ **Mac**: Command + Option + Left Arrow
- ● **Open a New Window**:
    - ○ **Windows**: Ctrl + N
    - ○ **Mac**: Command + N
- ● **Open Incognito Mode**:
    - ○ **Windows**: Ctrl + Shift + N
    - ○ **Mac**: Command + Shift + N
- ● **Navigate Back and Forward**:
    - ○ **Back**:
        - ■ **Windows**: Alt + Left Arrow
        - ■ **Mac**: Command + Left Arrow
    - ○ **Forward**:
        - ■ **Windows**: Alt + Right Arrow
        - ■ **Mac**: Command + Right Arrow

Address Bar Shortcuts

The address bar (or Omnibox) in Chrome is not just for entering URLs; it can also be used for various actions:

- **Search Google**: Type a search query directly into the address bar and hit Enter.
- **Access Bookmarks**: Type chrome://bookmarks in the address bar to quickly access your bookmarks.
- **Open History**: Type chrome://history to view your browsing history.
- **Directly Access Specific Sites**: You can type the first few letters of a bookmarked website and hit Enter to go directly to that site.

Productivity Tips

To maximise productivity while using Chrome, consider the following tips:

1. **Use Keyboard Shortcuts**: Familiarise yourself with the shortcuts mentioned above. The more you use them, the more

natural they will become, speeding up your workflow.

2. **Customise Shortcuts**: Chrome allows you to customise some keyboard shortcuts for extensions you have installed. You can access this feature by going to chrome://extensions/shortcuts in the address bar.

3. **Practice Regularly**: Regularly use these shortcuts in your daily browsing to build muscle memory, which will make you more efficient over time.

Using the Chrome Task Manager

Chrome's built-in Task Manager is an invaluable tool for monitoring resource usage and managing active processes. It provides insight into how each tab and extension consumes system resources, allowing you to optimise performance and troubleshoot issues.

Accessing Chrome Task Manager

To open the Chrome Task Manager, follow these steps:

- **Windows and Mac**: Press Shift + Esc while Chrome is open, or right-click on the Chrome title bar and select **Task Manager** from the context menu.

Understanding the Task Manager Interface

Once you open the Task Manager, you will see a list of all open tabs and extensions, along with the following columns:

- **Task**: The name of the tab or extension.
- **Memory**: The amount of RAM being used by each task, measured in kilobytes.
- **CPU**: The percentage of CPU resources used by each task.
- **Network**: The amount of network data sent and received by the tab.
- **Process ID**: The unique identifier for each task running in Chrome.

Managing Tasks

Using the Task Manager, you can perform
several actions:

- **End Task**: If a tab or extension is causing
  issues, you can select it and click the **End
  Process** button. This will immediately
  close the selected task, freeing up system
  resources.
- **Sort by Resource Usage**: Click on any
  column header (like Memory, CPU, or
  Network) to sort the tasks based on that
  metric. This helps you identify which tabs
  or extensions are consuming the most
  resources.

Tips for Using the Task Manager

1. **Monitor Performance**: Keep an eye on
   the Task Manager when you notice
   slowdowns in your browser. This will help
   you identify problematic tabs or
   extensions.
2. **Close Unused Tabs**: If you have multiple
   tabs open, consider closing the ones you're

not actively using to conserve memory
and CPU resources.

3. **Manage Extensions**: Some extensions
can be resource-heavy. Use the Task
Manager to identify which extensions are
using the most resources and consider
disabling or removing them if they're not
essential.

Saving Time with Tab Groups and Pinned Tabs

Effective tab management is crucial for
productivity in Chrome, especially when
juggling multiple projects or tasks. Chrome
offers features like Tab Groups and Pinned Tabs
that help you stay organised and reduce clutter.

1. Tab Groups

Tab Groups allow you to organise your tabs into
categories, making it easier to manage related
pages.

Creating a Tab Group

To create a tab group, follow these steps:

1. **Open Multiple Tabs**: Start by opening several tabs that you want to group together.
2. **Right-click on a Tab**: Choose one of the tabs you want to group and right-click on it.
3. **Select Add Tab to New Group**: This option will allow you to create a new group.
4. **Name Your Group**: You can assign a name and colour to your group for easier identification.
5. **Add More Tabs**: To add more tabs to the group, right-click on other tabs, select **Add to group**, and choose the group you just created.

Using Tab Groups

- **Collapse and Expand**: You can collapse a tab group to minimise the space it occupies, which helps keep your tab bar clean. Click on the group name to collapse or expand it.

- **Move Tabs Within Groups**: You can easily rearrange tabs within a group by dragging and dropping them.
- **Remove Tabs from Groups**: Right-click on a tab within a group and select **Remove from group** to take it out of the group.

2. Pinned Tabs

Pinned Tabs are another way to keep important websites readily accessible without cluttering your tab bar.

Pinning a Tab

To pin a tab:

1. **Right-click on the Tab**: Locate the tab you want to pin.
2. **Select Pin**: Click on the **Pin** option from the context menu.

Benefits of Pinned Tabs

- **Space Saving**: Pinned tabs take up less space on your tab bar, as they are displayed as icons only.
- **Always Available**: Pinned tabs remain open and are not affected when you close and reopen Chrome, ensuring you have quick access to frequently used sites, such as email or social media.
- **Prevent Accidental Closure**: Pinned tabs cannot be accidentally closed; you must right-click and select **Unpin** to remove them.

Troubleshooting and Maintenance

Maintaining optimal performance in Google Chrome is crucial for a smooth and efficient browsing experience. Despite its user-friendly design, users may encounter issues such as slow performance, crashes, or unwanted software that affects their browsing.

How to Speed Up Chrome Performance

Over time, Chrome may slow down due to accumulated browsing data, too many extensions, or resource-intensive tabs. Here are several strategies to enhance Chrome's performance:

1. Clear Browsing Data

Accumulated cache, cookies, and history can slow down Chrome. Clearing this data can help:

- **Open Settings**: Click on the three-dot menu in the upper right corner and select **Settings**.
- **Privacy and Security**: Navigate to the **Privacy and security** section.
- **Clear Browsing Data**: Click on **Clear browsing data**.
- **Select Data Types**: Choose the time range and the types of data you want to clear (e.g., browsing history, cookies, cached images).
- **Clear Data**: Click the **Clear data** button.

Regularly clearing your browsing data can significantly improve performance, especially if you browse frequently.

2. Manage Extensions

Extensions enhance Chrome's functionality, but having too many installed can slow it down. To manage extensions:

- **Access Extensions**: Type chrome://extensions in the address bar and hit Enter.
- **Review Extensions**: Disable or remove any extensions that you don't use regularly by toggling them off or clicking the **Remove** button.

3. Use the Chrome Task Manager

The Chrome Task Manager helps identify tabs and extensions consuming excessive resources:

- **Open Task Manager**: Press Shift + Esc or right-click on the title bar and select **Task Manager**.
- **Identify Resource Hogs**: Look for tabs or extensions using a lot of memory or CPU.
- **End Task**: Select any problematic task and click **End Process** to close it.

4. Update Chrome

Keeping Chrome updated ensures you have the latest performance enhancements and security fixes. Chrome typically updates automatically, but you can check for updates manually:

- **Go to Settings**: Click on the three-dot menu, select **Help**, and then **About Google Chrome**.
- **Update Chrome**: Chrome will check for updates and install them if available. After updating, restart the browser.

5. Disable Hardware Acceleration

Hardware acceleration can improve performance in some cases, but it might also cause issues. Disabling it may help:

- **Open Settings**: Click on **Settings**.
- **Advanced Settings**: Scroll down and click on **Advanced**.
- **System**: Under the **System** section, toggle off **Use hardware acceleration when available**.

- **Restart Chrome**: Close and reopen Chrome to apply changes.

6. Limit Open Tabs

Having too many open tabs can overwhelm Chrome's resources. Try to:

- **Close Unused Tabs**: Regularly review and close tabs you're not actively using.
- **Use Tab Groups**: Organise related tabs into groups to minimise clutter and make navigation easier.

Managing and Resolving Chrome Crashes or Freezes

Chrome may occasionally crash or freeze, which can be frustrating. Here are some strategies to troubleshoot and resolve these issues:

1. Check for Conflicting Software

Sometimes, other software installed on your computer can conflict with Chrome, leading to crashes. Google provides a built-in tool to identify problematic software:

- **Open Settings**: Click the three-dot menu and select **Settings**.
- **Advanced**: Scroll down and select **Advanced**.
- **Reset and Clean Up**: Go to the **Reset and clean up** section and click on **Clean up computer**.
- **Find Harmful Software**: Click **Find** to search for and remove any software that may be causing issues.

2. Disable Extensions

Extensions can sometimes lead to crashes or freezes. To check if this is the case:

- **Enter Incognito Mode**: Open Chrome in Incognito Mode (Ctrl + Shift + N). Extensions are disabled in this mode by default.
- **Observe Performance**: If Chrome runs smoothly in Incognito, one of your

extensions may be causing the issue. Go to chrome://extensions to disable extensions one by one and identify the culprit.

3. Update Graphics Drivers

Outdated graphics drivers can impact Chrome's performance:

- **Check for Updates**: Visit the website of your graphics card manufacturer (NVIDIA, AMD, Intel) to check for driver updates and follow their instructions for installation.

4. Restart Your Computer

If Chrome frequently crashes or freezes, restarting your computer can free up resources and resolve temporary issues affecting performance.

Updating Chrome to the Latest Version

Regular updates are crucial for maintaining Chrome's performance and security. To ensure you're running the latest version:

1. Automatic Updates

Chrome usually updates automatically. However, you can verify this:

- **Settings**: Click on the three-dot menu, select **Help**, then **About Google Chrome**. If an update is available, Chrome will download and install it automatically.

2. Manual Update

If you suspect your browser isn't up to date:

- **Check for Updates**: Follow the steps mentioned above to check for and apply updates.

3. Restart Chrome

After updating, ensure to restart Chrome to apply the latest changes effectively.

Resetting Chrome Settings and Removing Malware

If Chrome continues to exhibit problems, resetting its settings can help restore it to its original state without deleting your bookmarks or saved passwords. Here's how to reset settings:

1. Reset Chrome Settings

- **Open Settings**: Click on the three-dot menu and select **Settings**.
- **Advanced**: Scroll down and expand **Advanced** settings.
- **Reset and Clean Up**: Under the **Reset and clean up** section, click **Restore settings to their original defaults**.
- **Confirm Reset**: A confirmation dialog will appear. Click **Reset settings** to complete the process.

Resetting Chrome will revert all settings to their defaults and disable all extensions but will keep your data intact.

2. Remove Malware

If you suspect malware may be affecting Chrome's performance:

- **Clean Up Tool**: As mentioned earlier, use the **Clean up computer** tool in Chrome settings to scan for and remove harmful software.
- **Use Anti-Malware Software**: Consider running reputable antivirus or anti-malware software to conduct a full system scan.

Advanced Chrome Tips and Tricks

Google Chrome is not only a powerful web browser but also a versatile tool for developers and advanced users. This section explores several advanced tips and tricks, including the use of Developer Tools, creating web apps, exploring experimental features, and enabling offline browsing.

Using Developer Tools for Web Development

Google Chrome's Developer Tools (DevTools) are essential for web developers. These built-in tools provide a suite of features for inspecting and debugging web pages, optimising performance, and enhancing user experience. Here's how to get started with DevTools:

1. Accessing Developer Tools

- **Open DevTools**: You can access DevTools in several ways:
    - Right-click on a webpage and select **Inspect**.
    - Press Ctrl + Shift + I (or Cmd + Option + I on Mac).
    - From the menu, click on the three dots in the top right corner, select **More tools**, and then **Developer tools**.

2. Key Features of Developer Tools

- **Elements Panel**: This panel allows you to inspect and modify HTML and CSS in real-time. You can view the structure of a webpage, modify elements, and see the changes reflected immediately.

- **Console Panel**: The Console provides a command-line interface for executing JavaScript. It's useful for testing scripts and debugging. Errors and warnings in the code are also logged here.
- **Network Panel**: This panel tracks all network requests made by the page. It helps developers analyse load times, identify bottlenecks, and debug issues with resources like images, scripts, and stylesheets.
- **Performance Panel**: This feature allows developers to record the runtime performance of a page and identify potential performance issues. You can analyse frame rates, resource loading times, and CPU usage.
- **Application Panel**: Here, you can inspect resources like cookies, local storage, session storage, and service workers. It's essential for managing data storage in web applications.
- **Sources Panel**: This panel displays the JavaScript files that are loaded for the

page, allowing developers to set breakpoints for debugging and analysing scripts.

3. Mobile Device Simulation

DevTools allows you to simulate how a webpage appears on mobile devices:

- **Toggle Device Toolbar**: Click on the device icon (or press Ctrl + Shift + M) to switch to device mode.
- **Select Device**: Choose a specific device from the dropdown menu to see how your website looks on different screen sizes and resolutions.

4. Debugging JavaScript

To debug JavaScript using DevTools:

- **Set Breakpoints**: In the Sources panel, find the JavaScript file you want to debug. Click on the line number to set a breakpoint.

- **Step Through Code**: Use the debugging controls (step over, step into, step out) to navigate through your code and inspect variables in real-time.

Using Developer Tools effectively can significantly enhance the web development process, allowing for efficient debugging and performance optimization.

Creating Web Apps with Chrome

Google Chrome supports Progressive Web Apps (PWAs), which are web applications that offer native-like experiences on the web. Here's how to create and use web apps in Chrome:

1. What are Progressive Web Apps?

PWAs combine the best of web and mobile apps, offering features such as:

- **Offline Access**: PWAs can work offline or on low-quality networks, providing a seamless experience.
- **Home Screen Installation**: Users can install web apps on their devices, making them accessible like native apps.
- **Push Notifications**: PWAs can send notifications to engage users even when they are not actively using the app.

2. Creating a Progressive Web App

To create a PWA:

Service Worker: Implement a service worker, which is a script that runs in the background and enables offline capabilities, caching, and background sync.

```
// Registering a service worker
if ('serviceWorker' in navigator) {

navigator.serviceWorker.register('/service-worke
r.js')
        .then(registration => {
```

```
      console.log('Service Worker registered
with scope:', registration.scope);
   });
}
```

- **Web App Manifest**: Create a manifest file (manifest.json) that defines how your app appears on the user's home screen, including its name, icons, and theme colours.

```
  {
"name": "My Web App",
"short_name": "Web App",
"start_url": "/index.html",
"display": "standalone",
"icons": [
  {
    "src": "icon-192x192.png",
    "sizes": "192x192",
    "type": "image/png"
  },
  {
    "src": "icon-512x512.png",
```

```
    "sizes": "512x512",
    "type": "image/png"
  }
 ]
}
```

- **HTTPS Requirement**: Ensure your app is served over HTTPS, which is essential for security and for enabling service workers.

3. Installing a PWA

Once you have a PWA ready, users can install it directly from Chrome:

- **Install Button**: When users visit your web app, a button may appear in the address bar, allowing them to install the app on their devices.
- **Home Screen Icon**: After installation, the app can be accessed from the home screen, just like any other native app.

Creating web apps with Chrome provides a powerful way to reach users across different platforms while delivering a high-quality experience.

Exploring Chrome's Experimental Features (Chrome Flags)

Chrome allows users to access experimental features through "Chrome Flags." These features may not be stable but can enhance functionality and provide insights into upcoming capabilities.

1. Accessing Chrome Flags

To explore experimental features:

- **Open Flags Page**: Type chrome://flags in the address bar and hit Enter.

2. Navigating Chrome Flags

- **Search Functionality**: Use the search bar at the top to find specific flags by entering keywords related to the features you're interested in.

- **List of Flags**: You'll see a list of experimental features, each with a brief description. Flags are categorised into **Enabled**, **Disabled**, and **Default** states.

3. Enabling Experimental Features

To enable a flag:

- **Select a Flag**: Click the dropdown menu next to the flag you want to enable.
- **Change State**: Choose **Enabled** or **Disabled** based on your preference.
- **Relaunch Chrome**: After making changes, a prompt will appear to relaunch Chrome for the changes to take effect.

4. Notable Chrome Flags

Some popular experimental features include:

- **Tab Groups**: Organise tabs into groups for better management.
- **Lazy Loading**: Improve performance by loading images only when they come into the viewport.

- **Dark Mode**: Enable a dark theme for the browser interface.

Exploring Chrome Flags can be an exciting way to experiment with new features and improve your browsing experience.

Offline Browsing with Google Chrome

Offline browsing allows users to access web content even without an internet connection. Chrome supports this feature through caching and service workers.

1. Understanding Offline Capabilities

When using web apps that support offline functionality:

- **Cached Content**: The service worker caches resources, allowing users to view previously loaded pages and data without needing an internet connection.

- **Background Sync**: Changes made while offline can be synced once the connection is restored.

2. Accessing Cached Pages

To access cached pages when offline:

- **Visit Recently Loaded Pages**: If you have recently visited a page, you can access it without an internet connection by typing the URL in the address bar.
- **View Cached Content**: Some web applications allow users to view cached content, displaying a message indicating they are offline but can access saved information.

3. Using Chrome for Offline Reading

Chrome also allows users to save pages for offline reading:

- **Save Page for Offline Access**: Open a page you want to save, click the three-dot menu, and select **More tools**, then **Save**

page as. Choose **Webpage, Complete** to save all resources.

- **Access Offline Pages**: You can view saved pages by going to the **Downloads** section in Chrome or by using the saved file.

Offline browsing is a useful feature that ensures access to critical information when internet connectivity is unavailable.

Glossary of Terms

A

1. **Address Bar**: The text field in the browser where users can enter a URL or search query.
2. **Ad Blocker**: A browser extension that prevents advertisements from being displayed on web pages.
3. **Auto-fill**: A feature that automatically fills in forms and passwords based on saved data.

B

4. **Bookmark**: A saved link to a specific webpage for easy access later.

5. **Browser Extension**: A small software module that adds functionality to the browser.
6. **Cache**: Temporary storage used by the browser to speed up the loading of web pages.

C

7. **Chrome Flags**: Experimental features in Chrome that can be enabled for testing purposes.
8. **Cookies**: Small files stored on a user's device that save data related to web browsing sessions.
9. **Cross-Origin Resource Sharing (CORS)**: A security feature that allows or restricts resources requested from another domain.

D

10. **DevTools**: Developer tools in Chrome used for debugging and inspecting web pages.

11.   **Downloads**: Files that users save from the web to their devices through the browser.

E

12.   **Extensions**: Additional software components that enhance the functionality of the Chrome browser.

13.   **Incognito Mode**: A private browsing mode that does not save browsing history or cookies.

F

14.   **Favicon**: A small icon associated with a website, displayed in the browser's address bar and bookmarks.

15.   **Fillable Forms**: Online forms that allow users to input data.

G

16.   **Google Account**: A user account that allows access to various Google services, including syncing Chrome data.

17. **Home Page**: The default web page that opens when launching the browser.

H

18. **History**: A log of all web pages visited by the user.
19. **HTML (Hypertext Markup Language)**: The standard markup language used to create web pages.

I

20. **Incognito**: A browsing mode that prevents data from being saved during the session.
21. **Internet Protocol (IP)**: A numerical label assigned to each device connected to a computer network.

J

22. **JavaScript**: A programming language used to create interactive effects within web browsers.

K

23. **Keyboard Shortcuts**: Combinations of keys that perform specific functions within the browser.

L

24. **Links**: Hyperlinks that connect to other web pages or resources.
25. **Loading Time**: The amount of time it takes for a web page to fully load.

M

26. **Malware**: Malicious software designed to harm or exploit devices or networks.
27. **Menu**: A list of options or commands in the browser interface.

N

28. **Navigation Bar**: The part of the browser interface that allows users to

navigate back, forward, refresh, or go to the home page.

29.   **Network**: A group of interconnected devices that can communicate with each other.

O

30.   **Omnibox**: Chrome's address bar that combines the URL and search functionality.

31.   **Offline Mode**: A feature that allows access to previously visited pages without an internet connection.

P

32.   **Pop-ups**: New browser windows that open unexpectedly, often used for advertisements.

33.   **Progressive Web App (PWA)**: A web application that provides a native app-like experience.

34.   **Privacy Settings**: Options that allow users to control their data privacy and security in the browser.

Q

35.   **Query**: A search term entered into the address bar or search engine.

R

36.   **Refresh**: The action of reloading the current web page.

37.   **Resolution**: The amount of detail an image holds, commonly referred to in pixels for screens.

S

38.   **Search Engine**: A system designed to search for information on the web, like Google.

39.   **Service Worker**: A script that runs in the background and enables offline capabilities and caching.

40. **Settings**: The configuration options available to customise the browser experience.

T

41. **Tab**: An open webpage within the browser that can be switched between.
42. **Tab Management**: The ability to organise and handle multiple tabs efficiently.
43. **Task Manager**: A feature that displays the resources used by different tabs and extensions.

U

44. **URL (Uniform Resource Locator)**: The address used to access a specific webpage.
45. **User Agent**: A string that identifies the browser and operating system to websites.

V

46.   **Viewport**: The visible area of a webpage on a device's screen.

47.   **Virus**: Malicious software designed to replicate and spread to other devices.

W

48.   **Web App**: An application accessed via a web browser that provides functionality similar to desktop applications.

49.   **Web Browser**: A software application used to access and navigate the internet.

50.   **Web Development**: The process of creating and maintaining websites.

X

51.   **XML (Extensible Markup Language)**: A markup language used to define rules for encoding documents in a format readable by both humans and machines.

Y

52. **YouTube**: A video-sharing platform that can be accessed through Chrome.

Z

53. **Zoom**: The ability to increase or decrease the size of the content displayed in the browser.

Additional Terms (54-100)

54. **Accessibility**: Features and design considerations that make web content usable for people with disabilities.
55. **Adware**: Software that displays advertisements on your device, often bundled with other software.
56. **Analytics**: Tools that track and analyse web traffic and user behaviour.
57. **API (Application Programming Interface)**: A set of rules for building software applications, enabling

communication between different software components.

58. **Bookmark Bar**: A toolbar that displays saved bookmarks for quick access.

59. **Browser Cache**: Temporary storage that helps load previously visited pages faster.

60. **Browser History**: A record of all the pages a user has visited.

61. **Content Delivery Network (CDN)**: A network of servers that delivers web content to users based on their geographic location.

62. **CSS (Cascading Style Sheets)**: A style sheet language used for describing the presentation of a document written in HTML.

63. **Data Privacy**: The aspect of information technology that deals with the proper handling of data.

64. **Default Browser**: The browser that opens automatically when a user clicks on web links.

65. **DNS (Domain Name System)**: The system that translates domain names into IP addresses.

66. **Drag and Drop**: A user interface feature that allows users to click on an object and move it to a different location.

67. **File Download**: The process of saving a file from the web to your local device.

68. **Firefox**: A popular open-source web browser developed by Mozilla.

69. **Full-Screen Mode**: A viewing mode that expands the browser window to cover the entire screen.

70. **HTTPS (HyperText Transfer Protocol Secure)**: An extension of HTTP that secures communication over a computer network.

71. **Interactive Content**: Media that requires user interaction, such as quizzes and polls.

72. **Java**: A programming language often used for web development and creating applets.

73. **Load Time**: The time it takes for a web page to fully load.

74. **Malicious Software**: Software designed to harm, exploit, or otherwise compromise a system.

75. **Network Security**: Measures to protect a network from unauthorised access and attacks.

76. **Open Source**: Software with source code that anyone can inspect, modify, and enhance.

77. **Page Speed**: The time it takes for a webpage to display all of its content.

78. **PDF Viewer**: A feature or extension that allows users to view PDF documents in the browser.

79. **Phishing**: A fraudulent attempt to obtain sensitive information by disguising as a trustworthy entity.

80. **Query String**: A part of a URL that assigns values to specified parameters.

81. **Responsive Design**: An approach to web design that makes web pages render

well on a variety of devices and window or screen sizes.

82. **Scripting Language**: A programming language that is interpreted rather than compiled, often used in web development.

83. **Session**: A temporary connection established between a user and a web server.

84. **Shared Links**: URLs that can be shared with others to access specific web pages.

85. **Spam**: Unsolicited or irrelevant messages sent over the internet, often in bulk.

86. **SSL (Secure Sockets Layer)**: A standard technology for establishing an encrypted link between a server and a client.

87. **Tethering**: Sharing a mobile device's internet connection with another device.

88. **URL Shortener**: A service that creates a shorter version of a long URL for easier sharing.

89.   **User Experience (UX)**: The overall experience of a person using a website, especially in terms of how easy or pleasing it is to use.

90.   **User Interface (UI)**: The space where interactions between humans and machines occur.

91.   **Web Cache**: A mechanism for temporarily storing web documents to reduce server lag.

92.   **Web Hosting**: A service that allows individuals or organisations to post a website on the internet.

93.   **Web Server**: A server that stores and serves web pages to users over the internet.

94.   **WYSIWYG (What You See Is What You Get)**: An editor that allows users to see what the end result will look like while the document is being created.

95.   **XML Sitemap**: A file that lists the URLs for a site and helps search engines crawl the site effectively.

96. **Zen Mode**: A distraction-free browsing mode that hides all toolbars and menus.

97. **Zoom Function**: A feature that allows users to increase or decrease the size of text and images on a webpage.

98. **Browser Sync**: A feature that allows users to synchronise bookmarks, history, and settings across devices.

99. **Context Menu**: A menu that appears upon right-clicking, providing additional options.

100. **User Profiles**: Different profiles within Chrome that allow separate settings, bookmarks, and extensions for different users.

Google Chrome Made Easy

Google Chrome Made Easy

www.ingramcontent.com/pod-product-compliance
Lightning Source LLC
LaVergne TN
LVHW052100060326

832903LV00060B/2446